SUPERHEROES

Frances Ridley

RISING STARS

Rising Stars UK Ltd.
22 Grafton Street, London W1S 4EX
www.risingstars-uk.com

Helping Everyone Achieve

NASEN House, 4/5 Amber Business Village, Amber Close,
Amington, Tamworth, Staffordshire B77 4RP

Every effort has been made to trace copyright holders and obtain their permission for the use of copyright materials. The publisher will gladly receive information enabling them to rectify any error or omission in subsequent editions.

All facts are correct at time of going to press.

The right of Frances Ridley to be identified as the author of this work has been asserted by her in accordance with the Copyright, Design and Patents Act 1988.

Published 2008

Text, design and layout © Rising Stars UK Ltd.
Series Consultant: Lorraine Petersen
Cover design: Neil Straker Creative
Cover photograph: Alamy
Design: Geoff Rayner, Bag of Badgers
Editorial: Frances Ridley
Photographs:
AKG: 8, 10, 11, 23, 24, 27, 29, 30, 36
Alamy: 4, 25, 41
Kobal Collection: 16-17, 19, 34, 38, 39, 41, 47
VinMag Archive: 14, 19, 20, 32, 33, 34, 40, 42, 44, 46

British Library Cataloguing in Publication Data.
A CIP record for this book is available from the British Library.

ISBN: 978-1-84680-443-4

Printed by: Craftprint International Ltd, Singapore

CONTENTS

SUPERHEROES: THE BIG PICTURE

Superheroes have been saving the planet for over 70 years. They burst into action in comic books. Now they are TV and film stars, too.

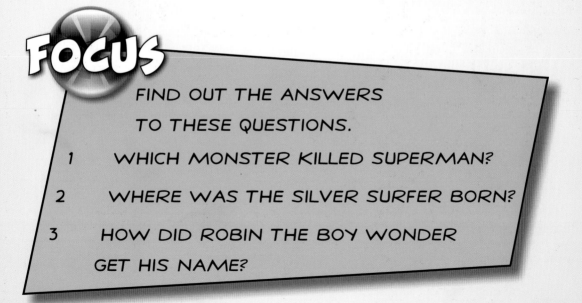

FOCUS

FIND OUT THE ANSWERS TO THESE QUESTIONS.

1   WHICH MONSTER KILLED SUPERMAN?

2   WHERE WAS THE SILVER SURFER BORN?

3   HOW DID ROBIN THE BOY WONDER GET HIS NAME?

ZOOMING IN...

Wonder Woman

Let's see what
a girl can do.

Batman

There's the bat signal
– it's time to fight crime!

Silver Surfer

It's never too late
to change your ways.

Superman
The ultimate superhero.

Spider-Man
This hero walks on walls.

The Hulk
Don't make him angry!

Superhero Teams
They work together
to fight crime.

HE CAME FROM OUTER SPACE

SUPERMAN WAS BORN ON THE PLANET KRYPTON.
HE WAS SENT TO EARTH IN A ROCKET.

SUPERMAN IS THE ULTIMATE SUPERHERO.
HE ALWAYS BEATS HIS ENEMIES.
HE HAS EVEN COME BACK FROM THE DEAD!

Fact File
Superman

PERSONAL DETAILS:
Place of birth: Planet Krypton
Address: The city of Metropolis, Earth
Age: About 30
Real name: Kal-El
Earth name: Clark Kent

Super-powers:
- Flying
- Super-vision and super-hearing
- Super-breath: my breath can freeze objects or blow them over
- Super-speed: I'm faster than a bullet
- Super-strength: I can lift a mountain

Weakness:

- Kryptonite radiation – it hurts me and stops my powers.

Background:

- I was sent to Earth from the Planet Krypton and was adopted by the Kent family.
- I got my super-powers when I was a teenager.
- I am a reporter on *The Daily Planet*.
- I'm married to Lois Lane – she also works for *The Daily Planet*.

RETURN FROM THE DEAD

In one story, Superman meets a monster called Doomsday.

Doomsday destroys things and kills people.

Superman and Doomsday have a battle.
They punch each other so hard that
both of them die! There is a big funeral for
Superman. But it's hard to get rid of
a superhero! Superman's body is put into
a special machine. The machine brings
Superman back to life. He's just in time to
save Metropolis – again!

TEENAGE HERO

SPIDER-MAN IS PETER PARKER IN EVERYDAY LIFE.

PARKER WAS A TEENAGER IN THE FIRST
SPIDER-MAN COMIC STORIES. IN LATER STORIES,
PARKER GETS A JOB AT A NEWSPAPER.
HE STILL TURNS INTO SPIDER-MAN WHEN
VILLAINS ARE ABOUT!

Peter Parker grew up with his Aunt and Uncle. He went to a science event when he was 15. A **radio-active** spider bit Parker. The bite gave him super-powers.

Parker has:

- super-strength and **agility**
- Spider Sense (he can tell what will happen before it happens)
- the power to walk up walls.

At first, Parker only used his powers to help himself and his family. Then, a robber ran past him. Parker didn't stop the robber. Later, the robber killed his Uncle. After that, Parker used his powers to fight crime. He became Spider-Man!

Planet Spider

Home

Shop

Life story

Info

Origin story

Adventures

Girlfriends

Enemies

Spider suits

THE SPIDER SUIT

The Spider suit helps Spiderman to fight crime.
It also has Spider tracers to track enemies and the
Spider signal – a powerful light.

WEB-BLASTERS – SHOOT OUT STICKY WEBS.

THE LIVING SUIT

In one story, Spider-Man's suit is torn to shreds. He finds a black and white spider-suit but the suit is an alien being!

It makes Spider-Man do things when he's asleep.

Spider-Man gets rid of the suit.

Eddie Brock finds it and puts it on.

The suit turns Brock into Venom – an evil villain.

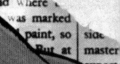

TEST DISASTER!

CLARK KENT AND PETER PARKER CAN TURN INTO SUPERHEROES. THEY DO THIS BECAUSE THEY WANT TO FIGHT VILLAINS.

DR BANNER IS NOT SO LUCKY.
HE TURNS INTO A MONSTER CALLED THE HULK – WHETHER HE WANTS TO OR NOT!

Dr Banner's Diary

Tuesday 1st

We are working on a Gamma bomb.
We're testing it tomorrow.

Wednesday 2nd

The bomb test was a disaster! I started the
countdown. Suddenly, I saw a teenager near
the bomb. I pushed him out of the way.
The bomb exploded and I was blasted with
gamma rays. I nearly died.

Monday 14th

The gamma rays have done something to me.
I keep turning into a monster called the Hulk.
Sometimes I can tell the Hulk what to do.
But sometimes he does what he wants.

Tuesday 15th

I've worked it out. I turn into the Hulk
when I get angry. I think the Hulk wants
to fight evil. Perhaps he will help people –
not hurt them.

SUPERHERO?

The Hulk has no super-powers
but he's very strong.

A CONTEST OF STRENGTH

In one story, the Hulk is sent into space. He has to fight a space weapon called Godseye. Godseye can match the strength of any other weapon. Godseye and the Hulk have a battle. Godseye can't match Hulk's strength and it explodes.

EDWARD **NORTON** LIV **TYLER** TIM **ROTH** WILLIAM **HURT**

FACT BOX

HIS STORY HAS STARRED IN TV SERIES AND FILMS.

CLOSE UP:
SUPERHERO TEAMS

The Fantastic Four got their powers when their spaceship crashed.

MR FANTASTIC

MAIN POWER: CHANGING HIS BODY SHAPE.

INVISIBLE WOMAN

MAIN POWER: MAKING HERSELF, OTHER PEOPLE AND THINGS INVISIBLE.

THING

MAIN POWER: SUPERHUMAN STRENGTH AND STAMINA.

HUMAN TORCH

MAIN POWER: COVERING HIS BODY WITH FIRE.

The Incredibles are a family of superheroes.

MR INCREDIBLE

MAIN POWER: SUPERHUMAN STRENGTH AND STAMINA.

ELASTIGIRL

MAIN POWER: CHANGING HER BODY SHAPE.

VIOLET

MAIN POWER: MAKING HERSELF INVISIBLE AND PUTTING UP FORCE FIELDS.

DASH

MAIN POWER: SUPER-SPEED.

THIS FAMILY OF SUPERHEROES WERE THE STARS OF THE 2004 FILM THE INCREDIBLES.

GOOD OR EVIL?

THE SILVER SURFER IS A POWERFUL SUPERHERO. HE CAN TRAVEL IN SPACE AND TIME. HE CAN GO FASTER THAN THE SPEED OF LIGHT. HE DOESN'T NEED TO EAT, DRINK OR SLEEP.

THERE'S JUST ONE PROBLEM. HE ISN'T ALWAYS ON THE GOOD SIDE.

"Galactus gave me some of his power and I turned into the Silver Surfer"

THE SILVER SURFER

Our reporter finds out the story behind the headlines.

Tell me about your early life.

I was born on Zenn-La. There was no crime, disease or hunger there.

A perfect planet!

Too perfect.
There was no need to fight. Then Galactus came in his spaceship. He wanted to destroy Zenn-La and feed on its energy.

What happened?

I made a deal. I agreed to find planets for Galactus. But he had to leave Zenn-La alone.

So you left Zenn-la?

Yes. Galactus gave me some of his power and I turned into the Silver Surfer. At first, I looked for planets with no people. Then Galactus **brain-washed** me.

I didn't care any more. I led Galactus to planets with people living on them…

A CHANGE OF HEART

In one story, the Silver Surfer leads Galactus to Earth. There is a battle between the Silver Surfer and The Fantastic Four. Then the Silver Surfer meets a blind woman. She senses that he is a good person. She begs him to turn away from Galactus. The Silver Surfer agrees. He helps The Fantastic Four to fight Galactus.

FILM FACT

THE 2007 FILM WAS BASED ON THIS STORY.
IN THIS FILM, THE SILVER SURFER'S POWER
COMES FROM HIS SURFBOARD.

THE MASKED MAN

BRUCE WAYNE SAW HIS PARENTS MURDERED BY A THUG. HE TOOK A VOW TO FIGHT CRIME. HE SPENT YEARS TRAINING HIS MIND AND BODY. NOW, WHEN THE BAT SIGNAL FLASHES, VILLAINS, BEWARE!

BATMAN'S PROMISE TO GOTHAM

Report by Alexander Knox
Picture by Vicki Vale

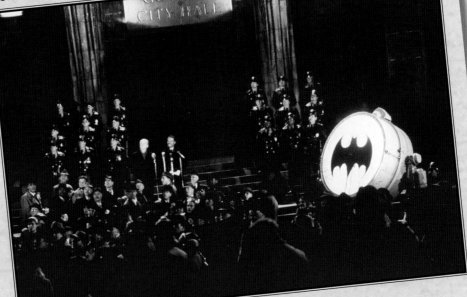

The Bat Signal

There were loud cheers yesterday for the new Bat Signal. It comes with a promise from Batman – he will defend Gotham City from crime!

BATMAN DEFEATS THE JOKER

Batman has already got rid of one criminal. The Joker was a horrible villain with white skin, green hair and an evil grin. He planned to kill thousands of people with a lethal gas.

Batman stopped him in his tracks. Then the Joker kidnapped Vicki Vale. He took her to the top of Gotham Cathedral. Batman and the Joker had a fight – and the criminal fell to his death! Who is Batman? Nobody knows. But the people of Gotham can sleep in peace now that Batman has made his promise!

Batman and the Evil Joker

INTO THE BAT CAVE

The batcave is Batman's HQ. He keeps his suit, gadgets and batmobile there. The Batsuit helps Batman to fight crime.

CAPE IS BULLET-PROOF AND FIRE-PROOF – IT IS ALSO A HANG-GLIDER!

BELT HOLDS USEFUL GADGETS.

BOOTS HAVE STEEL TOES.

Batman has had different batmobiles. This one is from the 1997 film *Batman and Robin*.

TAILFINS LOOK LIKE BAT'S WINGS

This batcycle is from the 1966 TV series.

ROBIN THE BOY WONDER

BAT FACT

ROBIN THE BOY WONDER WAS NAMED AFTER ROBIN HOOD.

GIRL POWER

WONDER WOMAN IS A DIFFERENT KIND
OF SUPERHERO. SHE WANTS TO SAVE THE
WORLD FROM HATRED AND WAR. SHE WANTS
TO TEACH PEOPLE LOVE AND PEACE.

SHE TALKS TO HER ENEMIES AND SHOWS THEM
A BETTER WAY TO LIVE. BUT SHE'S NO SOFTIE.
SHE FIGHTS HER ENEMIES IF SHE HAS TO
AND SHE ALWAYS WINS!

Current chat topic:

Is Wonder Woman the best superhero?

Started: Mar 11, 2008, 10.30 AM

Spacegirl   No, Superman is better. He even beat death!

So did Wonder Woman – in one story she dies and a goddess brings her back to life.   **Buzzer**

Spacegirl   Well Superman is stronger. And Batman has a better car!

Wonder Woman's got a car, a jet, a bike ...   **Twisted mind**

Reply

Buzzer

Yeah, she has a disk that can turn into any vehicle she needs.

But the vehicles are invisible! At least you can see the batmobile.

Spacegirl

Twisted mind

OK, what about the lasso of truth? Even Superman had to tell the truth when she got him with her lasso.

And no other hero has bullet-proof bracelets.

Buzzer

Spacegirl

They don't need them! Batman's cape is bullet-proof and bullets bounce off Superman. I still think Superman is better!

Reply

GIFTS FROM THE GODS

Wonder Woman's real name is Diana. She comes
from a tribe of women called the Amazons.
The Amazons are looked after by the gods.
The gods gave Diana many gifts. She is strong,
wise and beautiful. She can fly and talk to animals.
She's a skilled fighter.

LASSO OF TRUTH

BULLET-PROOF BRACELETS

The gods sent Diana to our world to fight for peace. She's a normal woman until she starts to spin. Then she turns into Wonder Woman!

GLOSSARY

Agility Spider-Man can move fast and easily.

Brain-washed Galactus makes the Silver Surfer forget his past.

Origin story All superheroes have an origin story. It shows how they get their powers.

Radio-active The spider got into an experiment with radio-active materials. The spider then gave its powers to Peter Parker when it bit him.

Tailfins The two back corners of Batman's car stick up like bat's wings. Tail fins were popular on 1950s cars.

INDEX